Crazy Sh*t
Republicans Say

Contents

INTRODUCTION 4
SARAH PALIN 22
GLENN BECK 56
MICHELE BACHMANN 66
COMMON ACTS OF ASININITY .79
ANN COULTER 122
WARNINGS FROM HISTORY 136
W 141
DICK 207
RICK PERRY 214
RELIGIOUS RIGHT 228
MICHAEL STEELE 244
RUSH LIMBAUGH 254
HERMAN CAIN 279
BILL O'REILLY 287
SEAN HANNITY 300

Liberals are pussies. Yes we all realize this. We gave them a majority in the House, the Senate, and even the Presidency. Only to be bullied out by a bunch of nut job community college dropouts that now control congress. Liberals are pussies, but at least they're not crazy or stupid… or worse, an incredibly dangerous hybrid of crazy-stupid known as the Tea Party. If you're reading this you're probably a liberal, or possibly a self-loathing conservative. Or maybe even Sean Hannity because you heard your name was mentioned in this book... In which case, Sean put the book down; you're not going to like it. If you are indeed a liberal, don't worry, you're in good company. Enjoy the ranks of such like-minded great men as Jesus Christ, Thomas Jefferson, John Adams, Benjamin Franklin, Abraham Lincoln, and Franklin Roosevelt. You might have noticed that many of these guys are the same "Founding Fathers" the Tea Party claims their ideals embody. At best, the only things they have in common are tri-corner hats.

I believe a great deal of people confuse being selfish, ignorant, and uncompassionate, with being conservative. Many people that call themselves "conservative" don't even know the actual political denotation of the word. So for their benefit I've included the definition.

con·serv·a·tive

    [kuhn-sur-vuh-tiv]

adjective

1. disposed to preserve existing conditions, institutions, or to restore traditional ones, and to limit change.

Now, after reading that, who in their right mind, would want to call himself or herself this? It's the opposite of progress. In fact, this is the opposite of the American Dream.

Just to further illustrate my point I've also included the definition of liberal.

lib·er·al

[lib-er-uhl, lib-ruhl]

adjective

1. favorable to progress or reform, as in political or religious affairs.

2. favorable to or in accord with concepts of maximum individual freedom possible, especially as guaranteed by law and secured by governmental protection of civil liberties.

3. favoring or permitting freedom of action, especially with respect to matters of personal belief or expression.

INTRODUCTION

So how did "liberal" become such a bad word? How did we let Republicans demonize the obviously superior political ideology? I'm guessing the fact that most liberals are pussies had something to do with it.

In fairness, the modern Republican party is basically an anti-intellectual, self-serving version of the modern Democratic. Both parties have a recent track record of big government, gross spending, and war. It's only a matter of what programs each party favors, which lobbies they cater to, and which social / economic strata are benefited that separates the two parties' initiatives.

Knowing that, I would think the average person would rather err on the side that favors social responsibility, intellectualism, truth, and equality. I mean, that would make sense... unless you're an asshole. In which case, you're probably a conservative.

This must end, seriously. We can not allow another generation to fall further into economic and social decay at the hands of a bunch of conservative retards (yes Sarah Palin, I said retards). We must unite and strike back at the neo-conservative juggernaut that is crippling mass media with atrocious moronic rants of falsehood that people are actually beginning to believe as facts. A balanced media bias is the stuff of pipe dreams, but we must strive to educate the masses about their despicable scheme.

INTRODUCTION

I propose implementing a strategy of identifying and ignoring crazy shit Republicans say. By ignoring the bull shit of the right, we can take it out of legitimate political discussion, and weaken its stranglehold on truth and progress. Be forewarned, Republicans are quite masterful at manipulating facts and spinning their righteously indignant lunacy.

They utilize several techniques in their evil ways. So I've compiled a list of common devices used by the right-wing to shock and stupefy the masses. The following conservative tactics should be memorized and re-taught to fellow non-idiots, so that they can be properly identified and ignored in the future.

Conservative Tactic # 1

"I know you are, but what am I?"

Conservatives desperately and continually create false connections with liberals to words and policy that are inherently part of the conservative agenda and culture. Examples include constantly labeling Democrats:

racist, ignorant, unpatriotic, corrupt, unethical, & fascist

In truth all of the horrible things listed above accurately apply to the definition of conservative that was previously listed. All of these terms and their respective meanings are aligned with the true conservative and right-wing ideology, and have absolutely nothing in common with liberal principles. This clever ruse is a very damaging trick and is by far the most common of all right-wing tactics. Conservatives epitomize hypocrisy with their extremes of unethical behavior. From gay sex scandals to extra marital affairs nobody does exactly what conservatives claim to condemn more than the GOP. Right-wingers now accuse liberals of being fascists. I guess they're assuming everyone forgot that fascism is a product of right-wing extremism, and it is evident in the writings and speeches of many conservative politicians and pundits. In fact the actions of Bush and his cabinet make it the most fascist administration in U.S. history.

Though liberals aren't allowed to have a negative view on the president, no matter how retarded (yep Sarah, I did it again) because that would make us unpatriotic. So no one is allowed to interrupt him fourteen times during interviews, shout "you lie" while he's addressing congress, call him the anti-Christ, or stick their finger in his face… unless of course they're a Republican.

INTRODUCTION

Conservative Tactic # 2

"Blame the Liberal Media"

The term *"Liberal Media"* is a lie. They claim everything that is not blatantly, if not shamelessly, right-wing propaganda, to be the work of the "Liberal Media." No, their news is 100% fair and balanced. Though, apparently offering the middle of the road opinion or explaining both sides of an issue is akin to communism. While there are several organizations that only push the conservative message, at the same time attacking progressives, most owned by News Corp… All we've got is **MSNBC**.

Conservative Tactic # 3

"We represent the middle class"

No you don't. Republican candidates represent "Crony Capitalism," which is the main reason the economy collapsed in 2008. The conservatives have recently adopted the trickery of attacking liberals by turning the phrase "Class Warfare" into something the Democrats are using against all the hard working simple Republican folk. This is actually exactly the opposite of the phrase's true meaning. Republican spin doctors have been advocating lower taxes, and what's more, that it's only fair that every American "contribute" their own share. The facts are that by year's end 2010 the U.S. medium annual wage was $26,364.

Compare that with Mitt Romney, who made over 42 million in the last two years. His tax rate in 2010 was only 13.9%. That sounds fair. And for all the Reaganites out there arguing for lower taxes, taxes are lower now than they were under Reagan. Our boy Mitt here would have paid 20-28% during the Reagan terms. Republicans began condemning Democrats for "Class Warfare" after a push to restore the former tax-rate of the 90's (when the economy was at its peak) from 35% to 39% which would only affect those who earn over $380,000. Oh by the way, that extra 4% from the richest Americans would protect Social Security and Medicare for the next 60 years. But the "Job Creators" didn't seem to care about programs that only benefited the middle class. Just makes you wonder, what's the 1% bitching about?

Conservative Tactic # 4

"Lie... a lot"

These guys love to just make shit up. Doesn't matter how far from reality the claim is, in fact the crazier the better. Whether it's about "Death Panels", Fascism, the scientific merit of "Intelligent Design," or Muslim schools in Kenya, rest assured, it's all total bullshit. To help you identify the most popular conservative threads of lies the following information is the actual truth:

- Only 2% of welfare recipients test positive for drug use
- The president is an American citizen
- Iraq was not connected with 9/11

INTRODUCTION

Conservative Tactic # 5

"God is on my side"

This claim is championed by brilliant leaders such as: George Bush, Tom DeLay, and Rick Perry. It's sad that they on some level actually believe this. The irony of this is Jesus was liberal, super liberal. Legislation on universal healthcare, education, equality, welfare, and abolishing the death penalty all seem to be the kind of stuff Jesus liked. Oh, and he definitely didn't like greedy rich dudes…
I believe he said something like:

"It is easier for a camel to go through the eye of a needle than for a rich man to enter the kingdom of God." MARK 10:25

Oh, snap. Sorry Romney, looks like you, and the entire Senate, are screwed. And so I send you out into the world armed with this knowledge to serve as a crusader for truth and justice.

Good luck and God speed.

INTRODUCTION

Who are you calling Liberal?

You can call Obama a lot of things. But he is not the liberal menace Fox News would have you believe. The Obama administration has deported over one million illegal aliens since he has taken office. He will have deported more illegal aliens in four years than the Bush administration did in eight. His administration has issued tens times more in fines to employers who hire undocumented workers. The military has grown every year under the current administration. Our Navy now is larger than the next 13 largest naval fleets combined. And Obama just ordered a bunch more ships. Taking into consideration that this president inherited the worst economic recession since the Great Depression, he has only spent around 1.5 trillion compared to the Bush administration's 5 trillion, most of which was spent on an unnecessary war in Iraq that has been proven to have absolutely nothing to do with the terror attacks on September 11th, 2001. Not to mention, the Iraq war has killed nearly 4,500 of our troops and seriously impaired for life countless others.

To be fair, Obama has killed some people too, namely terrorists. He ordered the attack on Osama Bin Laden's compound. In September 2011, Anwar al-Awlaki, the al Qaeda leader of the Arabian Peninsula was killed. In January 2012 Obama sent Seal Team Six into Somalia to rescue hostages from pirates who worked with local war lords. And just for good measure, he had the Seals kill the pirates too; after all, we could always use fewer pirates.

INTRODUCTION

"Not all conservatives are stupid, but all stupid people are conservative."

- H.L. Menckin

SARAH PALIN

"The America I know and love is not one in which my parents or my baby with Down Syndrome will have to stand in front of Obama's 'death panel."

- Sarah Palin, (08/07/09)

Sarah employs the baseless argument of the GOP, that somehow Healthcare Reform will lead to everyone pleading their case for assistance in front of a murderous "Death Panel". The appalling thing about this is that unlike this idiot, who somehow became the leader of Alaska, there are millions of Americans who have aging parents and children with serious health issues that cannot afford the outrageous cost of healthcare in this country.

"We used to hustle over the border for health care we received in Canada. And I think now, isn't that ironic?"

- Sarah Palin, (03/06/10)

Ha Ha, yes that is ironic…but also incredibly hypocritical and kind of makes you look like a real asshole. I guess Canada's socialized healthcare was good enough for your parents and children, but not America, huh? That is ironic.

Here, Sarah admits that her family used to sneak over the border to enjoy the wonderful services of Canada's single-payer healthcare system.

"He who warned, uh, the British that they weren't gonna be takin' away our arms, uh, by ringing those bells, and um, makin' sure as he's riding his horse through town to send those warning shots and bells that we were going to be sure and we were going to be free, and we were going to be armed."

- Sarah Palin, (06/03/11)

Palin botches the story of Paul Revere's midnight ride. It is important to note that the average 4th Grader could get the story right.

One if by land, two if by sea… there were two. "The British are coming, the British are coming, to arms, to arms!" You even might have had to memorize Henry Wadsworth Longfellow's poem *The Midnight Ride of Paul Revere* in school yourself.

TWO DAYS LATER:

"[Paul Revere] did warn the British. And in a shout-out, gotcha-type of question that was asked of me, I answered candidly. And I know my American history."

- Sarah Palin, (06/05/11)

Two days? Two days, Sarah? Nobody gets two days to prepare a defense for such a stupid comment. Especially considering that most Americans already think you're a complete moron. You had two days to learn the history of Paul Revere. Ask a campaign worker, ask a 4th grader, Google it, read the freaking plaque underneath the monument of Paul Revere you visited… anything. And yet you have the balls to stick to what you said as an accurate depiction of what we all had to learn a goddamn poem about. And as for the "gotcha-type" question… the reporter asked her:

"What have you seen so far today, and what are you going to take away from your visit?"

You know what Sarah; you have every right to take issue with that asshole.

"Polls are for strippers and cross-country skiers"

- Sarah Palin, (09/03/11)

Sarah addressing supporters at a Tea Party rally in Iowa…

"If we were really domestic terrorists, President Obama would want to be palling around with us."
- Sarah Palin, (08/02/11)

Here Sarah was responding to the rumor that Vice President Biden said the Tea Party was acting like "terrorists" in the midst of the debt ceiling standoff during which the Republicans in congress intentionally tried to default the United States ability to pay (mostly Bush's) debt owed to other nations. Biden didn't actually say this, but he would have certainly been justified in labeling anyone who endeavors to weaken America's standing a "Terrorist."

"I love that smell of the emissions!"
- Sarah Palin, (05/29/11)

Sarah, at a motorcycle rally in D.C., where she rode in on a Harley… This somehow explains everything. You have finally unveiled a reasonable explanation for your thoughts and actions. You like to huff auto emissions.

"Because of that one episode, that one episode, that would turn an issue into what it has become over the last two years. I think that's ridiculous. That's one of those things, where that issue...that I don't read, or that I'm not informed, it's one of those questions where I like to turn that around and ask the reporters, 'Why would it be that there is that perception that I don't read?'"

- Sarah Palin, (12/09/10)

I don't know either…

"I want to help clean up the state that is so sorry today of journalism. And I have a communications degree."

- Sarah Palin, (11/22/10)

Sarah used this occasion to further exemplify her mastery of the English language, and her ever deserving rank amongst professional journalists.

"I haven't heard the president state that we're at war. That's why I too am not knowing -- do we use the term intervention? Do we use war? Do we use squirmish? What is it?"

- Sarah Palin, (03/29/11)

Regarding the U.S. and NATO bombing of Libya…

"Especially within hours of a tragedy unfolding, journalists and pundits should not manufacture a blood libel that serves only to incite the very hatred and violence they purport to condemn. That is reprehensible."

- Sarah Palin, (01/12/11)

In the wake of the Arizona shootings…

"Blood Libel" refers historically to the murder of Christian babies by Jews. So bad word choice… but what is truly reprehensible is that you have the audacity to defend your ever harmful rhetoric that advocates violence and fosters hatred and resentment towards liberals and anyone that doesn't share your small-minded views and incredibly ignorant perceptions. Such behavior is the definition of fascism.

"Dr. Laura: don't retreat...reload! (Steps aside bc her 1st Amend.rights ceased 2exist thx 2activists trying 2silence "isn't American,not fair")"

- Sarah Palin, (08/18/10)

Nice… I can't think of a better thing to say, you should have thrown in your "Put them in the Cross-hairs" catch phrase too. I could kind of make sense of your argument that she is protected under her first amendment rights if she were an angry caller, but she is however the professional host of a nationally syndicated talk show. Dr. Laura used the "N-Word" on air 11 times in 5 minutes. Even if she were an African American woman… she should have resigned. But that's interesting that you cite her 1st Amendment rights, we'll have to revisit that.

"Ground Zero Mosque supporters: doesn't it stab you in the heart, as it does ours throughout the heartland? Peaceful Muslims, pls refudiate."

- Sarah Palin, (07/18/10)

First of all, congratulations on inventing the word: "refudiate." Secondly, what happened to all that 1st Amendment talk?

"Peaceful New Yorkers, pls refute the Ground Zero mosque plan if you believe catastrophic pain caused @ Twin Towers site is too raw, too real."

- Sarah Palin, (07/18/10)

"[Barack and Michelle Obama] have power in their words. They could refudiate what it is that this group is saying."
- Sarah Palin, (07/14/10)

On the NAACP claiming the Tea Party movement is based in racism…

Yes they could "refudiate", but then they would be lying.

> "'Refudiate,' 'misunderestimate,' 'wee-wee'd up.' English is a living language. Shakespeare liked to coin new words too. Got to celebrate it!"

- Sarah Palin, (07/18/10)

So you're saying what appears as illiteracy is really literary genius… Thank God! For a minute there we all thought you were retarded.

"We have a President, perhaps for the very first time since the founding of our republic, who doesn't appear to believe that America is the greatest earthly force for good the world has ever known."

- Sarah Palin, (06/30/10)

The rest of the free world spent a great deal of the last two centuries catching up with America, now almost every western democracy is more progressive than the U.S.. If the last decade has shown us anything, it's that we no longer are who everyone else is trying to be. It is true that militarily we are a force to be reckoned with, but our GDP will be surpassed by China by 2016. America needs to realize, that it is one great power among many, if it's ever to be number one again.

"This is Reagan country (applause). Yeah! And perhaps it was destiny that the man who went to California's Eureka College would become so woven within and inter-linked to the Golden State."

- Sarah Palin, (06/25/10)

Sarah speaking at California State University – Stanislaus…

Reagan's Eureka College is in Illinois.

"What the federal government should have done is accept the assistance of foreign countries, of entrepreneurial Americans who have had solution that they wanted presented ... The Dutch and the Norwegians, they are known for dikes and for cleaning up water and for dealing with spills."

- Sarah Palin, (06/15/10)

Yes the Dutch countries are very good at building dikes and levees to keep their coastline from being washed out to sea, but not so much for reversing the single greatest preventable eco-disaster to ever hit the Gulf region. I'm not sure she even considered the environmental impact of the spill, only how we can restore the white sandy beaches in time for Spring Break.

"Shoot, I must have lived such a doggoned sheltered life as a normal, independent American up there in the Last Frontier, schooled with only public education and a lowly state university degree, because obviously I haven't learned enough to dismiss common sense."

- Sarah Palin, (06/13/10)

If you omit the words "to dismiss common sense," this is the most honest statement she ever said.

"Extreme deep water drilling is not the preferred choice to meet our country's energy needs, but your protests and lawsuits and lies about onshore and shallow water drilling have locked up safer areas. It's catching up with you. The tragic, unprecedented deep water Gulf oil spill proves it."

- Sarah Palin, (06/02/10)

Sarah, blaming the disaster of the Gulf oil-spill on environmentalist…

"We're all Arizonans now."
- Sarah Palin, (05/15/10)

Defending Arizona's law cracking down on immigrants…

No, obviously we're not.

"Only dead fish go with the flow."
- Sarah Palin, (07/03/09)

Sarah said, while quitting…

"Go back to what our founders and our founding documents meant -- they're quite clear -- that we would create law based on the God of the bible and the Ten Commandments."

- Sarah Palin, (05/06/10)

Actually, they were quite clear that they only wanted the exact opposite of that.

"Energy," "budget" (crossed out), "tax cuts" and "lift American spirit."

These are the crib notes written on Palin's left hand during a speech at the Tea Party Convention, in which she criticizes President Obama for using teleprompters in his speeches. (02/07/10)

"I didn't really had a good answer, as so often -- is me. But then somebody sent me the other day, Isaiah 49:16, and you need to go home and look it up. Before you look it up, I'll tell you what it says though. It says, hey, if it was good enough for God, scribbling on the palm of his hand, it's good enough for me, for us. He says, in that passage, 'I wrote your name on the palm of my hand to remember you,' and I'm like, 'Okay, I'm in good company.'"

- Sarah Palin, (03/05/10)

Explanation Palin gives to press for the use of crib notes…

"They are kooks, so I agree with Rush Limbaugh. Rush Limbaugh was using satire ... I didn't hear Rush Limbaugh calling a group of people whom he did not agree with 'f-ing retards,' and we did know that Rahm Emanuel, as has been reported, did say that. There is a big difference there."

- Sarah Palin, (02/07/10)

Sarah, trying to justify why it's perfectly acceptable for Rush Limbaugh to call people "retards", but not Rahm Emanuel…

"Who calls a shot like that? Who makes a decision like that? It's a disturbing trend."
- Sarah Palin, (11/06/09)

Here Sarah trots out a conservative conspiracy theory that "In God We Trust" had been moved to the edge of all U.S. coins by President Obama, when in fact the change was made by President Bush in 2007, and was even reversed by congress before Obama was inaugurated in 2009.

"**How sad that Washington and the media will never understand; it's about country. And though it's honorable for countless others to leave their positions for a higher calling and without finishing a term, of course we know by now, for some reason a different standard applies for the decisions I make."**

- Sarah Palin, (07/04/09)

Because they weren't resigning for a Fox News show and Reality TV gig…

"Let me go back to a comfortable analogy for me - sports... basketball. I use it because you're naive if you don't see the national full-court press picking away right now: A good point guard drives through a full court press, protecting the ball, keeping her eye on the basket... and she knows exactly when to pass the ball so that the team can WIN."

- Sarah Palin, (07/03/09)

While issuing her resignation speech Sarah makes the analogy that she is a good point guard driving to the basket, but has to pass the ball to [**herself**] so that her team [**Republicans**] can win by her achieving higher office [**Fox News Deal**] by resigning as Governor.

"It may be tempting and more comfortable to just keep your head down, plod along, and appease those who demand: 'Sit down and shut up,' but that's the worthless, easy path; that's a quitter's way out."

- Sarah Palin, (07/03/09)

Here Sarah explains that not quitting her job as Governor is the "quitter's way out."

"Letterman certainly has the right to 'joke' about whatever he wants to, and thankfully we have the right to express our reaction. This is all thanks to our U.S. military women and men putting their lives on the line for us to secure America's Right to Free Speech - in this case, may that right be used to promote equality and respect."

- Sarah Palin, (06/16/09)

Sarah, once again demonstrating her astute understanding of the 1st Amendment…

"I'm like, OK, God, if there is an open door for me somewhere, this is what I always pray, I'm like, don't let me miss the open door. Show me where the open door is."

- Sarah Palin, (11/10/08)

Referencing running for national office...

GLENN BECK

"When you see the effects of what they're doing to the economy, remember these words: We will survive. No -- we'll do better than survive, we will thrive. As long as these people are not in control. They are taking you to a place to be slaughtered!"

- Glenn Beck, (11/03/09)

I'm not sure we're living in the same century (or dimension) as Glenn Beck.

"This president I think has exposed himself over and over again as a guy who has a deep-seated hatred for white people or the white culture....I'm not saying he doesn't like white people, I'm saying he has a problem. This guy is, I believe, a racist."

- Glenn Beck, (07/28/09)

"I haven't seen a half-monkey, half-person yet."
- Glenn Beck, (10/20/10)

Glenn Beck, calling evolution **"ridiculous"**…

"I went to the movie this weekend with a gun. And surprise, surprise, I didn't kill anybody!"

- Glenn Beck, (07/22/09)

And movie-goers everywhere feel much safer…

"I could give a flying crap about the political process ... We're an entertainment company."
- Glenn Beck, (04/2010)

And it really shows…

"When I see a 9/11 victim family on television, or whatever, I'm just like, 'Oh shut up' I'm so sick of them because they're always complaining."

- Glenn Beck, (09/09/05)

"I'm thinking about killing Michael Moore, and I'm wondering if I could kill him myself, or if I would need to hire somebody to do it. ... No, I think I could. I think he could be looking me in the eye, you know, and I could just be choking the life out."

- Glenn Beck, (05/17/05)

"You can get rich making fun of me. I know. I've made lots of money making fun of me."

- Glenn Beck

"So here you have Barack Obama going in and spending the money on embryonic stem cell research. ... Eugenics. In case you don't know what Eugenics led us to: the Final Solution. A master race! A perfect person. ... The stuff that we are facing is absolutely frightening."

- Glenn Beck, (03/09/09)

MICHELE BACHMANN

"But we also know that the very founders that wrote those documents worked tirelessly until slavery was no more in the United States. ... I think it is high time that we recognize the contribution of our forbearers who worked tirelessly -- men like John Quincy Adams, who would not rest until slavery was extinguished in the country."

- Michele Bachmann, (01/2011)

Actually they didn't work at all to end slavery. John Quincy Adams was not one of the Founding Fathers. He is the son of a Founding Father, and slavery was around for like another 50 years after him anyway. In fact most of the Founding Fathers owned slaves at some point. Three of the first four presidents owned slaves while in office, including:

George Washington: **The Father of our Country**
Thomas Jefferson: **Declaration of Independence**
James Madison: **The Father of the Constitution**

"I will tell you that I had a mother last night come up to me here in Tampa, Florida, after the debate. She told me that her little daughter took that vaccine, that injection and she suffered from mental retardation thereafter."

- Michele Bachmann, (09/12/11)

"Why should I go and do something like that? But the Lord says, 'Be submissive wives; you are to be submissive to your husbands."

- Michele Bachmann, (2006)

Bachmann explaining that tax law was not her choice in careers, but that her husband wanted her to do it…

So if you won the presidency, could you make decisions concerning national security, or would you have to check with your husband first?

"If we took away the minimum wage -- if conceivably it was gone -- we could potentially virtually wipe out unemployment completely because we would be able to offer jobs at whatever level."

- Michele Bachmann, (01/2005)

Bachmann outlining the Republican solution to the job crisis, just make former teachers, engineers, and bankers clean bathrooms and pick strawberries for $17 a day…

"Carbon dioxide is portrayed as harmful. But there isn't even one study that can be produced that shows that carbon dioxide is a harmful gas."

- Michelle Bachmann, (04/2009)

She's right. There is not "one" study that shows that shows that carbon dioxide is a harmful gas… There are hundreds of studies that show that carbon dioxide is a harmful gas.

"I find it interesting that it was back in the 1970s that the swine flu broke out under another, then under another Democrat president, Jimmy Carter. I'm not blaming this on President Obama, I just think it's an interesting coincidence."

- Michele Bachmann, (04/28/09)

The Swine Flu outbreak in the 1970's was in 1976 during the Gerald Ford (Republican) presidency.

"I don't know how much God has to do to get the attention of the politicians. We've had an earthquake; we've had a hurricane. He said, 'Are you going to start listening to me here?' Listen to the American people because the American people are roaring right now. They know government is on a morbid obesity diet and we've got to rein in the spending."

- Michele Bachmann, (08/2011)

Bachman insinuating the Earth Quakes and Hurricanes of 2011 were messages from God to Congress…

If this statement doesn't terrify you that not only was this woman a viable candidate for the presidency, but she still remains a member of congress, then something is wrong with you.

"Well what I want them to know is just like, John Wayne was from Waterloo, Iowa. That's the kind of spirit that I have, too."

- Michele Bachmann, (06/2011)

Bachman said this in an interview following the announcement of her presidential campaign in her hometown of, Waterloo, Iowa. What's wrong with this? Well John Wayne was born in Winterset, a town over three hours away. Although, there was a famous John Wayne that was from Waterloo, John Wayne Gacy the serial killer.

"A government takeover of health care is the crown jewel of socialism,"

- Michele Bachmann, (02/01/10)

It must also be the "crown jewel" of every civilized and developed nation on earth other than us, because they all do it.

"There are things that are wrong with Japanese health care, but people are afraid of voicing. 'Well why is that,' I asked. [He said], 'Because they know that would get on a list and they wouldn't get health care. They wouldn't get in. They wouldn't get seen. And so people are afraid. They're afraid to speak back to government. They're afraid to say anything.' Is that what we want for our future? That takes us to gangster government at that point!"

- Michele Bachmann, (02/01/10)

This unfounded claim was supposedly based on an anonymous Japanese man that approached Michele Bachmann in Washington. Because we all know that Japanese men with concerns about their home country's healthcare have no better person to turn to than a small minded fanatic that obviously knows nothing of Japan. While it's not likely that this Japanese man actually does exist, either way, Bachmann is flat out making false statements. The Japanese, like most modern developed countries, use a universal healthcare program that is widely admired by the public. Healthcare costs in Japan are among the lowest on the planet. This is even more impressive considering Japan is much older per capita than the U.S.. Unlike Bachmann I have a statement from an authenticated Japanese citizen who currently lives in Japan:

"The current healthcare system is good for families, students and workers alike."
- Narumi Kobayashi, Age 22, (02/23/12)

COMMON ACTS OF ASININITY

Asininity:

the quality of being asinine; stupidity combined with stubbornness

"I believe and I think the right approach is to accept this horribly created — in the sense of rape — but nevertheless a gift in a very broken way, the gift of human life, and accept what God has given to you. As you know, we have to, in lots of different aspects of our life. We have horrible things happen. I can't think of anything more horrible. But, nevertheless, we have to make the best out of a bad situation."

- Rick Santorum, (1/20/12)

Santorum, arguing against aborting a pregnancy after being raped and suggesting women "have to make the best out of a bad situation"…

"I believe we have more to fear from the potential of that bill passing than we do from any terrorist right now in any country."

- Virginia Foxx (R- NC), (11/02/09)

On Healthcare reform…

"I hope that's not where we're going, but you know if this Congress keeps going the way it is, people are really looking toward those Second Amendment remedies and saying my goodness what can we do to turn this country around? I'll tell you the first thing we need to do is take Harry Reid out."

- Sharron Angle, Nevada Tea Party Senate Candidate, (01/2010)

Here, Sharron Angle advocates an armed insurrection, and murdering Senator Harry Reid.

"I'm telling you that this works. You know, before we all started having health care, in the olden days, our grandparents, they would bring a chicken to the doctor. They would say, 'I'll paint your house.' I mean, that's the old days of what people would do to get health care with your doctors. Doctors are very sympathetic people. I'm not backing down from that system."

- Sue Lowden, Senate candidate in Nevada, (04/19/2010)

So as long as we remember to bring the appropriate livestock with us to the emergency room, we're going to be alright.

"Do you know, where does this phrase 'separation of church and state' come from? It was not in Jefferson's letter to the Danbury Baptists.... The exact phrase 'separation of Church and State' came out of Adolph Hitler's mouth, that's where it comes from. So the next time your liberal friends talk about the separation of Church and State, ask them why they're Nazis."

- Glen Urquhart, Tea Party Congressional Candidate from Delaware, (04/2010)

Well you're kind of right. The exact phrase is not in Jefferson's letter, but all of the words are, with the exact same well intentioned contextual meaning of "separation of church and state".

The original text reads:

"legislature should 'make no law respecting an establishment of religion, or prohibiting the free exercise thereof,' thus building a wall of **Separation between Church & State.***"*

He used the word "Between" not "of". You caught us. We liberals made the whole thing up. Actually the Supreme Court did, the phrase was quoted by the U.S. Supreme Court first in 1878, probably as an interpretation of the Constitution's position on this issue. After all, such things are their job.

"You know what, evolution is a myth. Why aren't monkeys still evolving into humans?"

- Christine O'Donnell, (10/15/98)

Well if you'd allow us to teach evolution in schools maybe you would know the answer. Monkeys are still evolving, and so are humans. Though we share a common genetic ancestor with some primates, humans (homo-sapiens) are a separate species all together. At some point in our evolutionary history our species divided and continued evolving on a different path of development than that of our primate cousins. They too continued to evolve, in response to the physical and social pressures of their environment. The modern human and monkey are examples of two different and still evolving species.

"We had no domestic attacks under Bush; we've had one under Obama."
- Rudy Giuliani, (01/08/10)

The extreme irony of the man the media dubbed: *"Mr. 9/11"* forgetting 9/11…

"This fellow here, over here with the yellow shirt, macaca, or whatever his name is. He's with my opponent. He's following us around everywhere. And it's just great. ... Let's give a welcome to macaca, here. Welcome to America and the real world of Virginia."

- George Allen (R-VA), Summer 2006

Here George Allen ridicules S.R. Sidarth, a 20 yr. old native Virginian. He is calling Sidarth "Macaca," an ethnic slur referring to an Asian monkey.

"Keep your government hands off my Medicare."

- Tea Party Member, (07/28/09)

In a town hall meeting in South Carolina on healthcare reform, a Tea Party protester said this apparently unaware that Medicare is a government created and controlled program.

"Isn't that the ultimate homeland security, standing up and defending marriage?"

- Rick Santorum, (07/2004)

"Hunger can be a positive motivator."

- Cynthia Davis (R-Missouri), (06/2009)

Representative Cynthia Davis suggesting that removing a program that feeds poor children will prompt them to find the jobs that have otherwise been eluding them…

"I think gay marriage is something that should be between a man and a woman."

- California Governor Arnold Schwarzenegger (08/27/03)

"I like the color red because it's a fire. And I see myself as always being on fire."

- California Governor Arnold Schwarzenegger (07/2006)

"It may come as a shock to you who live out in the real world, but occasionally we do something up here. Not often, I admit, but sometimes. For example, I think the House has passed National Peach Month so far this year and we expect to act on it soon."

- Bob Dole, 1982

"The New York Times and Washington Post are both infested with homosexuals themselves. Just about every person down there is a homosexual or lesbian."

- Jesse Helms, 1995

"If you don't hold us accountable, we'll do some real bad things in Washington, D.C."
- John Ensign (R-NV), (09/01/10)

Yep, later John Ensign was investigated by the Senate Ethics Committee concerning an affair he had with the wife of his co-chief of staff.

"What I don't like from the president's administration is this sort of, I'll put my boot heel on the throat of BP. I think that sounds really un-American in his criticism of business. I've heard nothing from BP about not paying for the spill. And I think it's part of this sort of blame-game society in the sense that it's always got to be someone's fault instead of the fact that sometimes accidents happen."

- Rand Paul (R-KY), (05/21/10)

Senator Paul defending BP as if they had dropped a glass of milk, shortly after the Gulf oil spill -- a catastrophic accident that was entirely their fault…

"I think to some extent Jon Stewart and [Stephen] Colbert are the same way. I think Jon Stewart's a bigot. I think he looks at the world through, his mom, who was a school teacher, and his dad, who was a physicist or something like that. Great, I'm so happy that he grew up in a suburban middle class New Jersey home with everything you could ever imagine ... I'm telling you that everybody who runs CNN is a lot like Stewart, and a lot of people who run all the other networks are a lot like Stewart, and to imply that somehow they, the people in this country who are Jewish, are an oppressed minority? Yeah."

- CNN's Rick Sanchez, (09/30/10)

Yeah, he got fired for that.

"We needed to have the press be our friend ... We wanted them to ask the questions we want to answer so that they report the news the way we want it to be reported."

- Sharron Angle (R-NV), Senate Nominee, (08/02/10)

Doesn't sound like Nazi's at all…

"The first thing that has to be done is secure the border ... East Germany was very, very able to reduce the flow. Now, obviously, other things were involved. We have the capacity to, as a great nation, secure the border. If East Germany could, we could."

- Joe Miller (R-AK), (10/17/10)

On how to deal with illegal immigrants…

"I've always been fascinated by the fact that here was a relatively small country that from a strictly military point of view accomplished incredible things."

- Rich Iott, (10/11/10)

Ohio Tea Party House candidate defending his extensive participation in Nazi re-enactments and the Waffen SS uniform he routinely wore…

"They were doing what they thought was right for their country."
- Rich Iott, (10/11/10)

Referring to the Nazis who served in the 5th SS Panzer Division Wiking...

Former House Republican leader Tom DeLay, CNN interview, (03/07/10):

DeLay: "There is an argument to be made that these extensions, the unemployment benefits, keep people from going and finding job. In fact there are some studies that have been done that show people stay on unemployment compensation and they don't look for a job until two or three weeks before they know the benefits are going to run out."

CNN's Candy Crowley: "People are unemployed because they want to be?"

DeLay: "Well, it is the truth. And people in the real world know it."

"These are beautiful properties with basketball courts, bathroom facilities, toilet facilities. Many young people would love to get the hell out of cities."

- Carl Paladino, (08/2010)

New York Tea Party candidate for Governor, Carl Paladino, laying out his plan to convert prisons into dormitories for Welfare recipients…

"Home to smug, self-important, pampered liberal elitists."

- Carl Paladino, (09/16/10)

Describing Manhattan…

"I never considered myself a maverick."

- John McCain, (04/2010)

Considered...

You based your entire presidential campaign on it!

"Oh gosh. Give me a specific one ... I'm very sorry right off the top of my head, I know that there are a lot but, uh, I'll put it up on my website I promise you."

- Christine O'Donnell, (10/13/10)

Christine unable to name a single Supreme Court case she does not agree with… Ironically, Sarah Palin couldn't answer this question either in her interview with Katie Couric.

"The Girl Scouts allow homosexuals and atheists to join their ranks, and they have become a pro-abortion, feminist training corps. If the Girl Scouts of America can't get back to teaching real character, perhaps it will be time to look for our cookies elsewhere."

Hans Zeiger (R-WA), (2004)

Still, a small price to pay for Thin Mints…

"We finally cleaned up public housing in New Orleans. We couldn't do it, but God did."

- Richard H. Baker (R-LA), (09/12/05)

In reference to hurricane Katrina…

"If it's inevitable, just relax and enjoy it."
- Clayton Williams (R-TX), (03/24/90)

Comparing bad weather to rape…

"So many minority youths had volunteered for the well-paying military positions to escape poverty and the ghetto that there was literally no room for patriotic folks like me in Vietnam."

- Tom DeLay, 1988 Republican Convention

Reported in the *Houston Press…*

"I do know that it's true that if you wanted to reduce crime, you could, if that were your sole purpose, you could abort every black baby in this country, and your crime rate would go down."

- Bill Bennett, Former Education Secretary, (09/28/05)

"Corporations are people, my friend... of course they are. Everything corporations earn ultimately goes to the people. Where do you think it goes? Whose pockets? Whose pockets? People's pockets. Human beings, my friend."

- Mitt Romney, (08/11/11)

"I should tell my story. I'm also unemployed."
- Mitt Romney, (06/16/11)

Romney, whose net worth is over $200 million, said this while speaking to a group of unemployed people in Florida.

"President Washington, President Lincoln, President Wilson, President Roosevelt have all authorized electronic surveillance on a far broader scale."

- Alberto Gonzalez, Attorney General, (02/06/06)

Fascinating, considering President Washington and President Lincoln didn't even have light bulbs or telephones…

"I saw the young man over there with eggs Benedict, with hollandaise sauce. And I was going to suggest to you that you serve your eggs with hollandaise sauce in hubcaps. Because there's no plates like chrome for the hollandaise."

- Mitt Romney, (06/2011)

Good one.

"I have two grandchildren – Maggie is 11, Robert is 9. I am convinced that if we do not decisively win the struggle over the nature of America, by the time they're my age they will be in a secular atheist country, potentially one dominated by radical Islamists and with no understanding of what it once meant to be an American."

- Newt Gingrich, (03/2011)

"The internet is not something you just dump something on. It's not a truck. It's a series of tubes. And if you don't understand, those tubes can be filled and if they are filled, when you put your message in, it gets in line and it's going to be delayed by anyone that puts into that tube enormous amounts of material, enormous amounts of material."

- Ted Stevens (R-AK), (06/28/06)

"We did not have a terrorist attack on our country during President Bush's term."
- Dana Perino, (11/24/09)

White House Press Secretary, also forgetting 9/11…

"The Soviet Union had a balanced budget."

- Tom DeLay, (12/12/03)

Well, good to know, but I'm not sure it worked out so well for them.

"Three years ago, in the midst of an economic crisis, a newly elected President Barack Obama stepped in with a bailout for the auto industry."

- Mitt Romney, (02/14/12)

Pump the brakes Mitt. Automaker bailouts began in the fall of 2008 with President Bush, who lent $17.4 billion to GM and Chrysler in an effort to protect over 1 million jobs that were on the chopping block if he didn't act. But I forgot you're the guy that loves firing people.

Ann Coulter

"My only regret with Timothy McVeigh is he did not go to the New York Times Building."

- Ann Coulter, (08/25/02)

Advocating violence…

"I don't really like to think of it as a murder. It was terminating Tiller in the 203rd trimester. ... I am personally opposed to shooting abortionists, but I don't want to impose my moral values on others."
- Ann Coulter, (06/22/09)

On the murder of Kansas abortion doctor George Tiller...

Again openly advocating violence towards others, who are practicing legal and court protected surgery because of a difference in religious beliefs... This religion inspired hatred and intimidation is exactly what the framers of the Constitution abhorred and feared.

"This is no time to be precious about locating the exact individuals directly involved in this particular terrorist attack. We should invade their countries, kill their leaders, and convert them to Christianity."

- Ann Coulter, (09/13/01)

Overlooking everything else that is detestable about this statement… Yeah, because it's not like Christians have ever committed atrocities in foreign lands.

"Marriage is not a civil right.
You're not black."

- Ann Coulter, (09/26/10)

Ann Coulter: **"You will find liberals always rooting for savages against civilization."**

Bill O'Reilly: **"They didn't root for the Nazis against civilization."**

Ann Coulter: **"Oh yes they did. ... It was only when Hitler invaded their precious Soviet Union that at the last minute they came in and suddenly started saying, 'Oh no, now you have to fight Hitler.'"**

(05/07/10)

"We need to execute people like (John Walker Lindh) in order to physically intimidate liberals."
- Ann Coulter, (01/2002)

Again advocating violence…

"...and of course there are the 39 million greedy geezers collecting Social Security. The greatest generation rewarded itself with a pretty big meal."

- Ann Coulter, (12/12/03)

"Even Hillary Clinton claimed to have unearthed some evidence that she was a Jew. And that, boys and girls, is how the Jews survived thousands of years of persecution: by being susceptible to pandering."

- Ann Coulter, (06/22/09)

"**Usually the nonsense liberals spout is kind of cute, but in wartime their instinctive idiocy is life-threatening.**"

- Ann Coulter, from *Treason: Liberal Treachery from the Cold war to the War of Terrorism*, (2003)

"Liberals hate religion because politics is a religion substitute for liberals and they can't stand the competition."

- Ann Coulter, from *Slander: Liberal Lies About the American Right*, (2002)

"Liberals don't believe there is such a thing as "fact" or "truth."

- Ann Coulter, from *Slander: Liberal Lies About the American Right*, (2002)

I think it's the other way around sweetheart.

"God gave us the earth. We have dominion over the plants, the animals, the trees. God said, 'Earth is yours. Take it. Rape it. It's yours."
- Ann Coulter, (06/20/2001)

"Liberals hate America, they hate flag-wavers, they hate abortion opponents, they hate all religions except Islam, post 9/11. Even Islamic terrorists don't hate America like liberals do. They don't have the energy. If they had that much energy, they'd have indoor plumbing by now."

- Ann Coulter, from *Slander: Liberal Lies About the American Right*, (2002)

Cleary, it seems all of the **HATE** is on your side of the table.

Warnings from the past...

"**When fascism comes to America it will be wrapped in a flag and carrying a cross.**"

- Sinclair Lewis

"Why, of course the people don't want war . . . but, after all, it is the leaders of the country who determine the policy, and it is always a simple matter to drag the people along, whether it is a democracy, or a fascist dictatorship, or a parliament or a communist dictatorship.

. . Voice or no voice, the people can always be brought to the bidding of the leaders. That is easy. All you have to do is to tell them they are being attacked, and denounce the pacifists for lack of patriotism and exposing the country to danger."

- Hermann Goering, while on trial in Nuremberg (1946)

Seems kind of relevant…

"Should any political party attempt to abolish social security, unemployment insurance, and eliminate labor laws and farm programs, you would not hear of that party again in our political history. There is a tiny splinter group, of course, that believes you can do these things. Among them are [a] few other Texas oil millionaires, and an occasional politician or business man from other areas. Their number is negligible and they are stupid."

- Dwight D. Eisenhower, (11/8/54)

Seems even more relevant…

"These are not bad people. All they are concerned about is to see that their sweet little girls are not required to sit in school alongside some big overgrown Negroes."

- Dwight D. Eisenhower (1954)

Ike, defending racial segregation after the Brown vs. Board of Education decision…

W.

"You know, one of the hardest parts of my job is to connect Iraq to the war on terror."

- George W. Bush, (09/06/06)

"For every fatal shooting, there were roughly three nonfatal shootings. And, folks, this is unacceptable in America. It's just unacceptable, and we're going to do something about it"

- President George W. Bush, (05/14/01)

"You teach a child to read, and he or her will be able to pass a literacy test."
- George W. Bush, (02/21/01)

Yep.

W.

"I'm the master of low expectations"
- George W. Bush, (06/04/03)

"I'm telling you there's an enemy that would like to attack America, Americans, again. There just is. That's the reality of the world. And I wish him all the very best."

- George W. Bush, (01/12/09)

W.

"In terms of the economy, look, I inherited a recession; I am ending on a recession."

- George W. Bush, (01/12/09)

Actually you inherited the country from the Clinton administration, which saw the longest period of economic expansion in U.S. history, as well as the lowest poverty rates in 35 years. Bush inherited a $236 billion budget surplus. And what did Bush do with all this? He created tax cuts that favored the wealthy, increased national debt, and weakened economic growth. Then for dessert, he started an unnecessary war and occupation of Iraq on which he spent more than any other president… ever.

Yes there was a small recession which began two months after Bush took office in March of 2001. But Bush didn't stop there. In all, America was in recession 22 months of the 96 months Bush was President. Bush did create 3 million net jobs, though that's 20 million less than how many Clinton did in the same period of time. Dubbya should just admit that he is just jealous of Clinton's 65% end-of-term approval rating.

"I guess it's OK to call the secretary of education here 'buddy.' That means friend."

- George W. Bush, (01/08/09)

"So I analyzed that and decided I didn't want to be the president during a depression greater than the Great Depression, or the beginning of a depression greater than the Great Depression."

- George W. Bush, (12/18/08)

Good decision.

W.

"People say, well, do you ever hear any other voices other than, like, a few people? Of course I do."

- George W. Bush, (12/18/08)

"I've abandoned free market principles to save the free market system."

- George W. Bush, (12/16/08)

"I've been in the Bible every day since I've been the president."
- George W. Bush, (11/12/08)

So that's where you were.

"I want to share with you an interesting program -- for two reasons, one, it's interesting, and two, my wife thought of it -- or has actually been involved with it; she didn't think of it. But she thought of it for this speech."

- George W. Bush, (10/21/08)

W.

"This thaw -- took a while to thaw, it's going to take a while to unthaw."

- George W. Bush, (10/20/08)

"I didn't grow up in the ocean -- as a matter of fact -- near the ocean -- I grew up in the desert. Therefore, it was a pleasant contrast to see the ocean. And I particularly like it when I'm fishing."

- George W. Bush, (09/26/08)

W.

"Anyone engaging in illegal financial transactions will be caught and persecuted."

- George W. Bush, (09/19/08)

"We're fixing to go down to Galveston and obviously are going to see a devastated part of this fantastic state."

- George W. Bush, (09/16/08)

Texans… an ever prideful bunch…

W.

"First of all, I don't see America having problems."
- George W. Bush, (08/10/08)

"I'm coming as the president of a friend, and I'm coming as a sportsman."
- George W. Bush, (07/30/08)

On attending the Olympics…

"There's no question about it. Wall Street got drunk -- that's one of the reasons I asked you to turn off the TV cameras -- it got drunk and now it's got a hangover. The question is how long will it sober up and not try to do all these fancy financial instruments."

- George W. Bush, (07/18/08)

"I think it was in the Rose Garden where I issued this brilliant statement: If I had a magic wand -- but the president doesn't have a magic wand. You just can't say, 'low gas.'"

- George W. Bush, (07/15/08)

W.

"And they have no disregard for human life."

- George W. Bush, (07/15/08)

Referring to Afghan fighters…

"The economy is growing, productivity is high, trade is up, people are working. It's not as good as we'd like, but -- and to the extent that we find weakness, we'll move."

- George W. Bush, (07/15/08)

Just weeks before the almost complete collapse of the U.S. banking system…

"Amigo! Amigo!"
- George W. Bush, (07/10/08)

Speaking to the Italian Prime Minister Silvio Berlusconi in Spanish...

"Goodbye from the world's biggest polluter."
- George W. Bush, (07/10/08)

Sounds like kind of a "dick" way to end his parting address at his final G-8 Summit, but when you consider that he also threw in a fist pump when he said it… It's awesome.

"Throughout our history, the words of the Declaration have inspired immigrants from around the world to set sail to our shores. These immigrants have helped transform 13 small colonies into a great and growing nation of more than 300 people."

- George W. Bush, (07/04/08)

"Should the Iranian regime-do they have the sovereign right to have civilian nuclear power? So, like, if I were you, that's what I'd ask me. And the answer is, yes, they do."

- George W. Bush, (07/02/08)

"But oftentimes I'm asked: Why? Why do you care what happens outside of America?"

- George W. Bush, (06/26/08)

"I remember meeting a mother of a child who was abducted by the North Koreans right here in the Oval Office."

- George W. Bush, (06/26/08)

W.

"Your eminence, you're looking good."
- George W. Bush, (06/13/08)

To Pope Benedict XVI…

(The Pope should be addressed as "Your Holiness")

"One of the things important about history is to remember the true history."
- George W. Bush, (06/06/08)

Or rather, the History…

"Let's make sure that there is certainty during uncertain times in our economy."

- George W. Bush, (06/02/08)

"We got plenty of money in Washington. What we need is more priority."

- George W. Bush, (06/02/08)

"And so the fact that they purchased the machine meant somebody had to make the machine. And when somebody makes a machine, it means there's jobs at the machine-making place."
- George W. Bush, (05/27/08)

Can't argue with that logic…

"I don't want some mom whose son may have recently died to see the commander in chief playing golf. I feel I owe it to the families to be in solidarity as best as I can with them. And I think playing golf during a war just sends the wrong signal."

- George W. Bush, (05/13/08)

W.

"So long as I'm the president, my measure of success is victory -- and success."

- George W. Bush, (04/17/08)

"Thank you, your Holiness. Awesome speech."
- George W. Bush, (04/15/08)

To Pope Benedict…

"Let me start off by saying that in 2000 I said, 'Vote for me. I'm an agent of change.' In 2004, I said, 'I'm not interested in change -- I want to continue as president.' Every candidate has got to say 'change.' That's what the American people expect."

- George W. Bush, (03/05/08)

"And so, General, I want to thank you for your service. And I appreciate the fact that you really snatched defeat out of the jaws of those who are trying to defeat us in Iraq."
- George W. Bush, (03/03/08)

To Army General Ray Odierno…

"A lot of times in politics you have people look you in the eye and tell you what's not on their mind."

- George W. Bush, (04/06/08)

"Wait a minute. What did you just say? You're predicting $4-a-gallon gas? ... That's interesting. I hadn't heard that."

- George W. Bush, (02/28/08)

W.

"I'm oftentimes asked, what difference does it make to America if people are dying of malaria in a place like Ghana? It means a lot. It means a lot morally, it means a lot from a -- it's in our national interest."

- George W. Bush, (02/20/08)

"There is no doubt in my mind when history was written, the final page will say: Victory was achieved by the United States of America for the good of the world."

- George W. Bush, (01/12/08)

W.

"I can press when there needs to be pressed; I can hold hands when there needs to be -- hold hands."

- George W. Bush, (01/04/08)

"One of the great things about books is, sometimes there are some fantastic pictures."
- George W. Bush, (01/03/00)

W.

"I know the human being and fish can coexist peacefully."
- George W. Bush, (09/29/00)

It's unclear whether President Bush is addressing people, fish, or both.

"I think I may need a bathroom break. Is this possible?"

- George W. Bush, (09/14/05)

In a note to passed to Secretary of State Condoleezza Rice during a U.N. Security Council meeting…

Better raise your hand, just to be safe.

"You work three jobs? ... Uniquely American, isn't it? I mean, that is fantastic that you're doing that."
- George W. Bush, (02/04/05)

President Bush, speaking to a divorced mother of three…

"Because the -- all which is on the table begins to address the big cost drivers. For example, how benefits are calculate, for example, is on the table; whether or not benefits rise based upon wage increases or price increases. There's a series of parts of the formula that are being considered. And when you couple that, those different cost drivers, affecting those -- changing those with personal accounts, the idea is to get what has been promised more likely to be -- or closer delivered to what has been promised.

Does that make any sense to you? It's kind of muddled. Look, there's a series of things that cause the -- like, for example, benefits are calculated based upon the increase of wages, as opposed to the increase of prices.

Continued-

Some have suggested that we calculate -- the benefits will rise based upon inflation, as opposed to wage increases. There is a reform that would help solve the red if that were put into effect. In other words, how fast benefits grow, how fast the promised benefits grow, if those -- if that growth is affected, it will help on the red."

- George W. Bush, (12/13/05)

Bush explains Medicare Drug Bill…

"There's an old saying in Tennessee -- I know it's in Texas, probably in Tennessee -- that says, fool me once, shame on -- shame on you. Fool me -- you can't get fooled again."

- George W. Bush, (09/17/02)

W.

"They want the federal government controlling Social Security like it's some kind of federal program."

- George W. Bush, (11/02/00)

"Africa is a nation with a lot of diseases."

- George W. Bush, (07/2003)

W.

"They misunderestimated me."
- George W. Bush, (11/06/00)

"**Rarely is the questioned asked: Is our children learning?**"

- George W. Bush, (01/11/00)

W.

"Our enemies are innovative and resourceful, and so are we. They never stop thinking about new ways to harm our country and our people, and neither do we."

- George W. Bush, (08/05/04)

"My answer is bring 'em on."
- George W. Bush, (07/02/03)

Bush challenging militants to attack U.S. forces...

W.

"Our enemies are innovative and resourceful, and so are we. They never stop thinking about new ways to harm our country and our people, and neither do we."

- George W. Bush, (08/05/04)

"There ought to be limits to freedom."

- George W. Bush, (05/26/99)

"If this were a dictatorship, it would be a heck of a lot easier, just so long as I'm the dictator."

- George W. Bush, (12/18/00)

"You don't get everything you want. A dictatorship would be a lot easier."

- George W. Bush, (07/1998)

"I don't know where bin Laden is. I have no idea and really don't care. It's not that important. It's not our priority."

- George W. Bush, (3/13/02)

It's cool, the next guy will get him.

"Hmmm, uhh, hah -- ummm -- I, the answer is -- I haven't really thought of it that way, heh, heh. Heh. Here's how I think of it. Ummm -- heh heh. First I've heard of that, by the way, I, ah -- uhh -- the, uhh -- I, I guess I'm more of a practical fella. Uhh. I vowed after September the 11th that I would do everything I could to protect the American people. And, uhh -- my attitude, of course, was affected by the attacks.ha ha ...ummm Let me see... I knew we were at a war. I knew that the enemy, obviously, had to be sophisticated, and lethal, to fly hijacked airplanes, uhh, into -- facilities that would, we would, killing thousands of people, innocent people, doin' nothing, just sittin' there goin' to work."

- George W. Bush, (03/20/06)

The previous paragraph was Bush's verbatim response to the question:

"Do you believe this, that the war in Iraq and the rise of terrorism are signs of the apocalypse? And if not, why not?"

This response, which didn't even answer the question, took Bush 73 seconds to mutter out.

"I think I was unprepared for war."
- George W. Bush, (12/01/08)

Really, you don't say?

DICK

"Conservation may be a sign of personal virtue, but it is not a sufficient basis for a sound, comprehensive energy policy."
- Dick Cheney, (04/30/01)

After all, why try to conserve something we're running out of.

"**Principle is OK up to a certain point, but principle doesn't do any good if you lose."**

- Dick Cheney, White House Chief of Staff, 1976

"We also have to work the dark side, if you will. We have to spend time in the shadows. It's going to be vital for us to use any means at our disposal."
- Dick Cheney, (09/16/01)

I knew he was related to Darth Vader some how.

"Don't quote me on this, okay? I don't want to be quoted on this, so don't quote me - Sometimes the truth is so precious, it must be accompanied by a bodyguard of lies."

- Dick Cheney, (09/25/01)

He so quoted you…

"Go fuck yourself."
- Dick Cheney, (06/22/04)

Dick, being a dick to Senator Patrick Leahy on the Senate floor, during a discussion about the war profiteering of Halliburton…

"That's sort of the best thing I ever did."

- Dick Cheney, (04/22/10)

Dick's less than remorseful view on telling Senator Patrick Leahy to "go fuck yourself"…

RICK PERRY

"From time to time there are going to be things that occur that are acts of God that cannot be prevented."

- Texas Gov. Rick Perry, (05/03/10)

This is Perry's explanation of the entirely preventable Gulf oil spill disaster, as an "act of God." A more suitable example of an act of God would be Rick Perry being elected President.

"Texas is a unique place. When we came in the union in 1845, one of the issues was that we would be able to leave if we decided to do that. You know, my hope is that America and Washington in particular pays attention. We've got a great union. There is absolutely no reason to dissolve it. But if Washington continues to thumb their nose at the American people, you know, who knows what may come out of that?"

- Rick Perry, (04/15/09)

Perry suggesting the possibility of Texas seceding from America...
(because it worked out so well for them the last two times they tried it)

"If this guy prints more money between now and the election. I don't know what y'all would do to him in Iowa, but we -- we would treat him pretty ugly down in Texas. Printing more money to play politics at this particular time in American history is almost treacherous -- or treasonous in my opinion."

- Rick Perry, (08/15/11)

Perry, suggesting Federal Reserve Chairman Ben Bernanke is virtually guilty of treason…

"I don't think the federal government has a role in your children's education."

- Rick Perry, (08/15/11)

"Young Hispanics in Texas can aspire to be the next Rolando Pablos, the chairman of the Texas racing commission; maybe the next Roberto de Hoyos, who heads our economic development shop; and one of my favorites, the head of the Texas Alcoholic Beverage Commission Jose Cuevas. Is that awesome? That is the right job for that man."

- Rick Perry, (06/23/11)

Perry making a super tactful joke about Jose Cuervo brand tequila at a Latino convention in Texas…

**"You can always follow
me on Tweeter."**

- Rick Perry, (06/21/11)

"I think in America from time to time we have to go through some difficult times — and I think we're going through those difficult economic times for a purpose, to bring us back to those Biblical principles of you know, you don't spend all the money. You work hard for those six years and you put up that seventh year in the warehouse to take you through the hard times. And not spending all of our money. Not asking for Pharaoh to give everything to everybody and to take care of folks because at the end of the day, it's slavery. We become slaves to government."

- Rick Perry, (06/2011)

What version of the Bible do you have?

"Juarez is reported to be the most dangerous city in America."
- Rick Perry, (02/28/11)

Rick, forgetting that Juarez is across the Texas border in Mexico… But of course, it is unreasonable for us to expect the Governor of Texas to know which cities are in his state and which are in other countries.

"I am a firm believer in intelligent design as a matter of faith and intellect, and I believe it should be presented in schools alongside the theories of evolution."

- Rick Perry, 2010

As quoted in the San Angelo *Standard-Times*

No it should not. Intelligent Design is not science, it's a Creationist arranged rationalization for how organisms have come to exist based on a Deity. Creationism is religion and not science; therefore it has no place in a science classroom. Intelligent Design is not only un-scientific, when it's taught in public schools, it's unconstitutional.

"Even if an alcoholic is powerless over alcohol once it enters his body, he still makes a choice to drink. And, even if someone is attracted to a person of the same sex, he or she still makes a choice to engage in sexual activity with someone of the same gender."

- Rick Perry, from his book: *On My Honor*, 2008

"George W. Bush did a incredible job in the presidency, defending us from freedom."

- Rick Perry, (11/04/10)

Yes he did… yes he did.

"Is it the Mitt Romney that was on the side of — against the Second Amendment before he was for the Second Amendment? Was it — was before — he was before the social programs from the standpoint of — he was for standing up for Roe v. Wade before he was against first — Roe v. Wade?"

- Rick Perry, (09/22/11)

Rick trying his darndest to attack Mitt Romney during a GOP presidential debate… It's okay Rick, slow down and use your big boy words.

"It's a theory that's out there. It's got some gaps in it. In Texas we teach both Creationism and evolution."

- Rick Perry, (08/18/11)

Rick Perry's response to a child who asked if he believed in evolution…

RELIGIOUS RIGHT

"The feminist agenda is not about equal rights for women. It is about a socialist, anti-family political movement that encourages women to leave their husbands, kill their children, practice witchcraft, destroy capitalism and become lesbians."

- Pat Robertson, (07/1992)

"They intend to vote on the Sabbath, during Lent, to take away the liberty that we have right from God. This is an affront to God."

- Steve King (R-Iowa), (03/18/10)

Isn't this really just about you being pissed off you have to come into work on the weekend?

"The abortionists have got to bear some burden for this because God will not be mocked. And when we destroy 40 million little innocent babies, we make God mad. I really believe that the pagans, and the abortionists, and the feminists, and the gays and the lesbians who are actively trying to make that an alternative lifestyle, the ACLU, People for the American Way — all of them who have tried to secularize America — I point the finger in their face and say 'you helped this happen.'"

- Jerry Falwell, (09/13/01)

Jerry Falwell blaming the atrocities of 9/11 on America's secular ways... just two days after the attacks...

"Maybe we need a very small nuke thrown off on Foggy Bottom to shake things up"

- Pat Robertson, (10/09/03)

"God is the one who chooses our rulers."

- Katherine Harris (R-Fl), (08/22/06)

Explaining why **"the separation of church and state"** is "a lie"...

Harris also said: **"If you are not electing Christians, then in essence you are going to legislate sin."**

"**We don't have to protect the environment; the Second Coming is at hand.**"

- James Watt (Former Sec. of the Interior), (05/24/81)

"George Bush was not elected by a majority of the voters in the United States, he was appointed by God."

- William G. Boykin, (10/27/03)

I still want a recount.

"You're telling me that's in the First Amendment?"

- Christine O'Donnell, (10/18/10)

Here Christine questions whether the Constitution establishes separation of church and state during a debate in front of an audience of law students at Widener University Law School, most of whom immediately burst into laughter. Apparently they had actually read the Constitution.

RELIGIOUS RIGHT

"I had surgery and I can't lift luggage. That's why I hired him."
- Rev. George Rekers, Religious Right Co-founder of the Family Research Council (05/04/10)

In the Miami airport after returning from a 10 day romantic European getaway with a hired male prostitute…

"I don't know that atheists should be considered citizens, nor should they be considered patriots. This is one nation under God."
- George H. Bush, (08/27/88)

A more accurate statement would be that anyone who says atheists should not be considered citizens or patriots should not be considered patriots themselves, but rather fascist dick heads. The Pledge of Allegiance did not add the phrase "Under God" until 1954, in the peak of the McCarthyism era.

During the "Red Scare" congress and President Eisenhower sought to institute an ideological divide between "godless" Communism and a paranoid America. In doing so both the president and congress broke their oaths of office, "to support and defend the Constitution of the United States…". The establishment clause of the First Amendment clearly states:

"Congress shall make no law respecting an establishment of religion, or prohibiting the free exercise thereof…"

This is exactly what happens when the fascist viewpoints of McCarthyism, the Religious Right, or a Bush are allowed to govern over the majority.

"American scientific companies are cross-breeding humans and animals, and coming up with mice with fully functioning human brains."
Christine O'Donnelle, (11/15/07)

Oh if this were only true, how awesome the possibilities.

"It may be a blessing in disguise. ... Something happened a long time ago in Haiti, and people might not want to talk about it. Haitians were originally under the heel of the French. You know, Napoleon the third, or whatever. And they got together and swore a pact to the devil. They said, we will serve you if you will get us free from the French. True story. And so, the devil said, okay it's a deal. Ever since they have been cursed by one thing after the other."

- Pat Robertson, (01/13/10)

Pat's not-so-Christian view on the earthquake in Haiti that killed tens of thousands of people…

"Our school systems teach the children that they are nothing but glorified apes who are evolutionized out of some primordial soup of mud."

- Tom DeLay, (06/17/99)

Tommy boy said this on the floor of the U.S. House of Representatives, blaming the tragic shootings at Columbine on the teaching of evolution.

"Good Christians, like slaves and soldiers, ask no questions."

- Jerry Falwell, (12/1999)

MICHAEL STEELE

"Not in the history of mankind has the government ever created a job."

- Michael Steele, (02/02/09)

So who paid you when you were the Lieutenant Governor of Maryland?

"... is just a wish list from a lot of people who have been on the sidelines for years.. to get a little bling, bling."

- Michael Steele, (02/09/09)

Referring to the stimulus package…

"It will come to the table with things that will surprise everyone - off the hook."
- Michael Steele, (02/19/09)

Steele explaining how the RNC will use hip hop to seduce younger voters…

"Could you help a brother out? No more national conventions with 36 people of color in the room."
- Michael Steele, (04/08/09)

Steele's way of asking Florida to send some minority delegates to conventions… I guess he doesn't realize that there aren't too many minority Republicans (especially in the South).

"Rush Limbaugh is an entertainer. Rush Limbaugh — his whole thing is entertainment. He has this incendiary — yes, it's ugly."

- Michael Steele, (02/28/09)

Steele explains, on the D.L. Hughley show, that it's Rush's prerogative to agitate and be controversial…

"My intent was not to go after Rush - I have enormous respect for Rush Limbaugh. I was maybe a little bit inarticulate. ... There was no attempt on my part to diminish his voice or his leadership."
- Michael Steele, (03/04/09)

Steele quickly apologizing to Rush Limbaugh…

"The mice who are scurrying about the Hill are upset because they no longer have access to the cheese, so they don't know what's going on."
- Michael Steele, (03/11/09)

Steele's odd mice analogy to why several GOP leaders want him to step down…

"Yeah. I mean, again, I think that's an individual choice."
- Michael Steele, (03/2009)

Michael affirming his Pro-choice position in GQ…

"I am pro-life, always have been, always will be. I tried to present why I am pro-life while recognizing that my mother had a 'choice' before deciding to put me up for adoption."
- Michael Steele, (03/12/09)

Michael immediately backtracking from his Pro-choice position…

Michael Steele quotes from his 'favorite book', 'War and Peace':

***"It was the best of times;
it was the worst of times."***
- Michael Steele, (01/03/11)

At the 2011 RNC Chair Debate, when Steele was asked what his favorite book was he immediately said, "War and Peace." Then he began to recite the opening passage of the "The Tail of Two Cities."

RUSH LIMBAUGH

"We've already donated to Haiti. It's called the U.S. income tax."
- Rush Limbaugh, (01/13/10)

Here Rush brazenly discourages his listeners from donating to the relief efforts in Haiti after a devastating earthquake.

"Obama's got a health care logo that's right out of Adolf Hitler's playbook ... Adolf Hitler, like Barack Obama, also ruled by dictate."

- Rush Limbaugh, (08/06/09)

"Exercise freaks ... are the ones putting stress on the health care system."

- Rush Limbaugh, (06/12/09)

"Feminism was established so as to allow unattractive women easier access to the mainstream of society."

- Rush Limbaugh, (08/12/05)

"I'm a huge supporter of women. What I'm not is a supporter of liberalism. Feminism is what I oppose. Feminism has led women astray. I love the women's movement -- especially when walking behind it."

- Rush Limbaugh, (02/03/10)

Rush defending against criticism that he is a sexist…

"Take that bone out of your nose and call me back."

- Rush Limbaugh, (10/08/90)

Clearly he's not a racist either.

"So the only real question is, if Al Qaeda's active and capable, what are they going to do? Because we know what they want: they want Kerry, they want the Democrats in power. They'd love that. I'm not guessing."

- Rush Limbaugh, (3/15/04)

In an al Qaeda letter that surfaced the same month, the terror organization made it quite clear they supported Bush's reelection. It said it preferred Bush to Kerry because it was impossible to find a leader "more foolish" than Bush. The letter goes on to say, "Kerry will kill our nation while it sleeps because he and Democrats have the cunning to embellish blasphemy and present it to the Arab and Muslim nation as civilized…".

- Reuters, (03/17/04)

"What better way to head off more oil drilling, nuclear plants, than by blowing up a rig? I'm just noting the timing, here."

- Rush Limbaugh, (04/29/10)

Rush implying that "environmentalist whackos" blew up the oil rig in the Gulf that led to one of the largest environmental disasters in U.S. history and killed eleven people, to halt offshore drilling…

"Too many whites are getting away with drug use...Too many whites are getting away with drug sales...The answer is to go out and find the ones who are getting away with it, convict them, and send them up the river, too."

- Rush Limbaugh, (10/05/95)

"I am addicted to prescription pain medication."
- Rush Limbaugh, (10/10/03)

Rush admitting that he himself is a drug addict…

Can we convict you and send you up the river now?

"Guess what? Faisal Shahzad is a registered Democrat. I wonder if his SUV had an Obama sticker on it."

- Rush Limbaugh, (05/04/10)

Rush lying about the would-be Times Square bomber, who was in fact not a registered voter…

"He is exaggerating the effects of the disease. He's moving all around and shaking and it's purely an act. ... This is really shameless of Michael J. Fox. Either he didn't take his medication or he's acting."

- Rush Limbaugh, (10/23/06)

Rush referring to a commercial featuring Michael J. Fox in which Fox endorses Senator McCaskill for her support of embryonic stem cell research…

"The ocean will take care of this on its own if it was left alone and left out there. It's natural. It's as natural as the ocean water is."

- Rush Limbaugh, (05/03/10)

Rush's intelligent analysis of the Gulf oil spill…

"Do you know we have more acreage of forest land in the United States today than we did at the time the Constitution was written?"

- Rush Limbaugh, (02/18/94)

"Look, let me put it to you this way: the NFL all too often looks like a game between the Bloods and the Crips without any weapons. There, I said it."

- Rush Limbaugh, (01/19/07)

"Our politically correct society is acting like some giant insult's taken place by calling a bunch of people who are retards, retards...There's going to be a retard summit at the White House."

- Rush Limbaugh, (02/03/10)

See, Rush gets to say retard!

"The Phony Soldiers"
- Rush Limbaugh, (09/26/07)

This is the label Rush places on members of the military that didn't support the war in Iraq.

Funny thing, you see I was a member of the Army (155th Infantry Regiment). Though I was a proud, proficient, and disciplined Soldier, I disagreed with the war in Iraq. I wasn't alone. Several, usually the more intelligent, Soldiers objected to serving in Iraq with good cause. After a minimal amount of research and just plain common sense, many Soldiers like me realized that Iraq had absolutely nothing to do with 9/11, al Qaeda, or any terrorists other than the ones we created by destroying their country.

The Iraq war and our mission was a lie. I enlisted to pay for my education not to act as a private army serving crony capitalists. I love America, and I want to protect my country, and I would gladly fight and die doing just that. Iraq had nothing to do with defending freedom, and to ask a Soldier to give their life for anything less than that is disgraceful.

Fun Fact:

Neither Rush, O'Reilly, or Hannity ever served in the military.

"You know, this is all BS, as far as I'm concerned. Cross species evolution, I don't think anybody's ever proven that. They're going out of their way now to establish evolution as a mechanism for creation, which, of course, you can't do."

- Rush Limbaugh, (05/19/09)

"When do we ask the Sierra Club to pick up the tab for this leak?"

- Rush Limbaugh, (05/17/10)

Suggesting the environmental group the Sierra Club is responsible for the Gulf oil spill, due to their opposition of land drilling…

"That cracker made a lot of African-American millionaires."

- Rush Limbaugh, (07/13/10)

On the death of Yankees owner George Steinbrenner…

"This will play right into Obama's hands. He's humanitarian, compassionate. They'll use this to burnish their, shall we say, 'credibility' with the black community -- in the both light-skinned and dark-skinned black community in this country. It's made-to-order for them. That's why he couldn't wait to get out there, could not wait to get out there."

- Rush Limbaugh, (01/13/10)

Referring to Haiti earthquake relief...

"[Obama] wouldn't have been voted president if he weren't black. Somebody asked me over the weekend why does somebody earn a lot of money have a lot of money, because she's black. It was Oprah. No, it can't be. Yes, it is. There's a lot of guilt out there, to show we're not racists, we'll make this person wealthy and big and famous and so forth.... If Obama weren't black he'd be a tour guide in Honolulu or he'd be teaching Saul Alinsky constitutional law or lecturing on it in Chicago."

- Rush Limbaugh, (07/06/10)

"Not one Republican voted for this bailout. Remember way back in the fall, not one Republican voted for the TARP bailout?"

- Rush Limbaugh, (03/18/09)

He's right, one Republican didn't vote for the TARP bailout, 125 Republicans voted for the TARP Bill. Then President Bush, a Republican, signed it into law.

HERMAN CAIN

"I didn't know I was a conservative when it didn't matter to me growing up."

- Herman Cain

"I'm not a professional politician. I'm a professional problem solver, and I believe we should cut the salaries of senators and congressmen 10 percent until they balance the budget. I call that conservative common sense."

- Herman Cain

I actually don't disagree with this.

"The way to connect with voters on the plan is to simply give the facts. Fifty per cent of taxpayers pay 97 per cent of the taxes. By most people's standards, that's already fair. The President is playing the class warfare card because he knows that a lot of people may never hear that particular fact. But it's a fact."

- Herman Cain, (09/22/11)

Cain misstating the facts as it was the Republicans in congress that were first to declare Class Warfare…

"Engage the people. Don't try to pass a 2,700 page bill – and even they didn't read it! You and I didn't have time to read it. We're too busy trying to live – send our kids to school. That's why I am only going to allow small bills – three pages. You'll have time to read that one over the dinner table. What does Herman Cain, President Cain talking about in this particular bill?"

- Herman Cain, (06/07/11)

"First of all, I don't even know what Sim City is. Okay? I don't even know what it is. Secondly, it's a lie. That's all I can say. I don't even know what SimCity is."

- Herman Cain, (10/19/11)

Here Herman denounces claims that his famous "999" plan came from the popular video game Sim City, where the same tax structure is implemented on player's incomes. Herman however, does not deny his admiration and passion for Pokémon.

"We don't need to rewrite the Constitution of the United States of America, we need to reread the Constitution and enforce the Constitution. ... And I know that there are some people that are not going to do that, so for the benefit of those who are not going to read it because they don't want us to go by the Constitution, there's a little section in there that talks about 'life, liberty and the pursuit of happiness...'"

"Don't stop there, keep reading. Cause that's when it says 'when any form of government becomes destructive of those ideals, it is the right of the people to alter or abolish it.'"

- Herman Cain, (05/21/11)

Herman Cain, lecturing on how Americans need to re-read the Constitution, while citing phrases from the Declaration of Independence…

BILL O'REILLY

"So anyway I'd be rubbing your big boobs and getting your nipples really hard, kinda' kissing your neck from behind...and then I would take the other hand with the falafel thing and I'd just put it on your p***y but you'd have to do it really light, just kind of a tease business..."

- Bill O'Reilly, 2004

The above quote appears in the transcript from a sexual harassment suit filed against him by a Fox News co-worker.

"And guys, if you exploit a girl, it will come back to get you. That's called 'karma.'"

- Bill O'Reilly, 2004, "The O'Reilly Factor For Kids"

Bill O'Reilly:

"If the Taliban government of Afghanistan does not cooperate, then we will damage that government with air power, probably. All right? We will blast them, because..."

Sam Husseini, Institute for Public Accuracy:

"Who will you kill in the process?"

Bill O'Reilly:

"Doesn't make any difference."

The O'Reilly Factor, Fox News Channel, (09/13/01)

"If the Americans go in and overthrow Saddam Hussein and it's clean, he has nothing, I will apologize to the nation, and I will not trust the Bush Administration again, all right?"

- Bill O'Reilly, (03/18/03)

O'Reilly's promise to America…

"I was wrong. I am not pleased about it at all and I think all Americans should be concerned about this...What do you want me to do, go over and kiss the camera?"
- Bill O'Reilly, (02/10/04)

Worlds worst apology on ABC's "Good Morning America" after no weapons of mass destruction were found in Iraq…

"You know what's really frightening? You actually have an influence on this presidential election. That is scary, but it's true. You've got stoned slackers watching your dopey show every night and they can vote."

- Bill O'Reilly, (09/22/04)

To "Daily Show" host Jon Stewart…

"The 'shut up' line has happened only once in six years."
- Bill O'Reilly, (11/15/02)

Actually it's been used quite a bit, so much so that there are several clever video montages of O'Reilly using his favorite two words on YouTube.

"That's my advice to all homosexuals, whether they're in the Boy Scouts, or in the Army or in high school: Shut up, don't tell anybody what you do, your life will be a lot easier."

- Bill O'Reilly, (7/7/00)

Bill O'Reilly
Professor
(Of 12th Century Science)

O'Reilly's astute argument for the evidence of a higher power:

"I say listen, sun goes up, sun goes down. Tide comes in, tide comes out. There's no miscommunication."

- (5/9/2007)

"Tide goes in, tide goes out. Never a miscommunication."

- (1/4/2011)

"Sun comes up, the sun goes down. The tide comes in, the tide goes out. It always happens. Never a miscommunication."

- (1/5/2011)

"How'd the Moon get there? Look, you pinheads who attacked me for this, you guys are just desperate. How'd the Moon get there? How'd the Sun get there? How'd it get there? Can you explain that to me? How come we have that, and Mars doesn't have it? Venus doesn't have it. How come? Why not? How'd it get here?"

- Bill O'Reilly, (01/26/11)

Well, Mars actually has two moons. The Sun comes up and goes down frequently yes… because the earth rotates around the Sun while also revolving on its own axis. The gravitational pull of the moon controls our tides world wide.

Believe it or not, if you read this information from the elementary school text books it can all be found in, you might abandon your "Can't explain it, God did it!" views on our ever understandable universe.

America was founded during the Enlightenment when men came to the realization that the entire universe can be understood using reason, and that the "Old-World" crutch of religion was only necessary for matters of personal faith. It's not that the intellectual faculties of man have been reversed in the last 240 years. It's that even though narrow comprehension of proven physical science was rejected at public forums in the 18th Century, it's now being sponsored by right-wing television networks.

Sean Hannity

I take the greatest issue with those who, through organized and intentional efforts, spread idiocy to the ignorant and naïve. Ignorance is by far America's greatest hurdle to overcome and the largest issue we face as a nation. This section's quotes could just as easily be called a collection of lies.

Sean Hannity is 1 of 3 things:

1. Insane
2. Stupid
3. Liar

Of course there's the possibility that he's 2 out of 3.

"You're not listening, Susan. You've got to learn something. He had weapons of mass destruction. He promised to disclose them. And he didn't do it. You would have let him go free; we decided to hold him accountable."

- Sean Hannity, (4/13/04)

This, like a great deal of what Sean says, is completely untrue and just another example of a right-wing pundit trying to justify the war in Iraq.

More than six months before this statement David Kay (Bush Administration Weapons Inspector) testified that his team had:

"Not uncovered evidence that Iraq undertook significant post-1998 steps to actually build nuclear weapons or produce fissile material."

He also said they did not discover any chemical or biological weapons what so ever.

"Colin Powell just had a great piece that he had in the paper today. He was there [in Iraq]. He said things couldn't have been better."

- Sean Hannity, (9/19/03)

More Hannity bullshit…

This is actually what Colin Powell said:

"Iraq has come very far, but serious problems remain, starting with security. American commanders and troops told me of the many threats they face--from leftover loyalists who want to return Iraq to the dark days of Saddam, from criminals who were set loose on Iraqi society when Saddam emptied the jails and, increasingly, from outside terrorists who have come to Iraq to open a new front in their campaign against the civilized world."

- Colin Powell, (09/19/03)

"And in northern Iraq today, this very day, al Qaeda is operating camps there, and they are attacking the Kurds in the north, and this has been well-documented and well chronicled. Now, if you're going to go after al Qaeda in every aspect, and obviously they have the support of Saddam, or we're not."

- Sean Hannity, (12/9/02)

Hannity trying to further the delusion of a link between al Qaeda and Saddam, citing a speech where Dick Cheney outright lied to the American people…

Here's some more testimony from David Kay, Bush's Weapon Inspector:

"But we simply did not find any evidence of extensive links with al Qaeda, or for that matter any real links at all."

Hannity also adds the fabrication that al Qaeda was attacking the Kurds. The Kurds were being attacked in the late 90's by Saddam; at least until President Clinton began an extensive two year air strike campaign to destroy Saddam's ability to harm his own people.

Unlike Bush, Clinton did not find it necessary to invade and destroy an entire country, kill tens of thousands of innocent civilians, kill 4,500 U.S. troops, and thrust America into generations of debt.

"[After 9/11], liberal Democrats at first showed little interest in the investigation of the roots of this massive intelligence failure...[Bush and his team] made it clear that determining the causes of America's security failures and finding and remedying its weak points would be central to their mission."

- Sean Hannity, (2002), "Let Freedom Ring"

Actually, Bush opposed the creation of the 9/11 commission. In May of 2002, he publically opposed a commission probe on how the government responded to terror threats before 9/11, despite the insistence to do so by those same "liberal Democrats."

Now Sean, just because you say something over and over again doesn't make it true.

"First of all, this president -- you know and I know and everybody knows -- inherited a recession...it was by every definition a recession"

- Sean Hannity, (11/6/02)

"Now here's where we are. The inherited Clinton/Gore recession. That's a fact."

- Sean Hannity (5/6/03)

"The president inherited a recession."

- Sean Hannity, (7/10/03)

"He got us out of the Clinton-Gore recession."

- Sean Hannity, (10/23/03)

"They did inherit the recession. They did inherit the recession. We got out of the recession."

Sean Hannity, (12/12/03)

"And this is the whole point behind this ad, because the president did inherit a recession."

- Sean Hannity, (1/6/04)

"Historically in every recovery, because the president rightly did inherit a recession. But historically, the lagging indicator always deals with employment."

- Sean Hannity, (1/15/04)

"Congressman Deutsch, maybe you forgot but I'll be glad to remind you, the president did inherit that recession."

- Sean Hannity, (1/20/04)

"He did inherit a recession, and we're out of the recession."

- Sean Hannity, (2/2/04)

"The president inherited a recession."

- Sean Hannity, (2/23/04)

"The president inherited a recession."

- Sean Hannity, (3/3/04)

"Well, you know, we're going to show ads, as a matter of fact, in the next segment, Congressman. Thanks for promoting our next segment. What I like about them is everything I've been saying the president ought to do: is focusing in on his positions, on keeping the nation secure in very difficult times, what he's been able to do to the economy after inheriting a very difficult recession, and of course, the economic impact of 9/11."

- Sean Hannity, (3/3/04)

"All right. So this is where I view the economic scenario as we head into this election. The president inherited a recession."

- Sean Hannity, (3/16/04)

"First of all, we've got to put it into perspective, is that the president inherited a recession."

- Sean Hannity, (3/26/04)

"Clearly, we're out of the recession that President Bush inherited."

- Sean Hannity, (4/2/04)

"Stop me where I'm wrong. The president inherited a recession, the economic impact of 9/11 was tremendous on the economy, correct?"

- Sean Hannity, (4/6/04)

"[President George W. Bush] did inherit a recession."

- Sean Hannity, (5/3/04)

"[W]e got [the weak U.S. economy] out of the Clinton-Gore recession."

- Sean Hannity, (5/18/04)

"We got out of the Clinton-Gore recession."

- Sean Hannity, (5/27/04)

"We got out of the Clinton-Gore recession."

- Sean Hannity, (6/4/04)

Like I said, you can say something over and over again (and Sean Hannity does), but it doesn't make it true. The Clinton – Gore recession Hannity continues to praise Bush for rescuing us from is really the Bush – Cheney recession. The recession according to the National Bureau of Economic Research began in March of 2001, two months after the start of Bush's first term. Not to mention, there were over 120,000 jobs added to the U.S. economy during the two months before the recession began. Besides the fact that this particular recession was the shallowest in modern history, Hannity certainly enjoyed spinning Clinton's legacy of eight years of massive growth into the economic problems that Bush "inherited."

Please vote or I will be forced to write:

Crazy Sh*t Democrats Do.
^
don't